RELEASE & SURRENDER
It's Your Turn For A Miracle

DEBORAH NAONE

Book cover photo credit: Justin Luebke

Dedication & Gratitude

Cole and Drue,
Who inspire me to be the best Mom and person I can possibly be. Who journeyed alongside me through good times and difficult times; always bearing the gifts of love and laughter. Who have the uncanny ability to find the silver lining in most everything. Two precious souls whom I am grateful to God for putting in my care, long enough to discover that it was they who were teaching me some of life's most valuable lessons.

My Parents,
Who have loved and supported me on my journey and never lost faith that I would find my place in the world and succeed in doing what I love. Their wellspring of support will be treasured for Eternity.

Erkan,
To whom I am forever grateful. Who was there for me in Ireland in a time of self- healing, discovery, and breakthroughs in consciousness. Who taught me, by example, what it is to truly give. Whose presence gave me a safe place to rest and be my authentic self and then allowed me to go back home... renewed and reenergized... to pursue my purpose and mission.

My Revelation~

God is with me.
For me.
Works through me.
As close as my breath.
God breathes me.

ACKNOWLEDGEMENTS

I give thanks and would like to express gratitude to the following Spiritual Leaders and Thought Leaders dedicated to the mastery of their spiritual craft. Some have passed on and some continue to blaze the trail on the leading edge of thought. The following people whose teachings or programs I have learned from and have contributed in some way to the writing of this book:

Kahlil Gibran, Lao Tzu, Albert Einstein, Mahatma Gandhi, Dr. Wayne Dyer, Caroline Myss, Doreen Virtue, Deepak Chopra, Stephen R. Covey, Eckhart Tolle, Marianne Williamson, Gary Zukav, Nick Bunick, Derek Rydall, John Assaraf,

Oprah Winfrey, Hay House, Louise Hay & Reid Tracy for countless inspirational works.

Plus inspiration that comes from the teachings of
The Christ that walked the Earth
And his Mother Mary

NOTE FROM THE AUTHOR

This is not a book about religion. I personally don't subscribe to any one religion. There are truths that exist in various religions that I hold dear. And the truth is, Love is my religion.

I don't believe in a Hell below. The only hell I believe in is the hell we create for ourselves in the here and now...when we lose sight of who we really are and why we're here.

I do believe in miracles, miracles that can only come from a Source greater than ourselves. Miracles that come when we make the decision to release & surrender.

In our human pursuit to seek meaning and purpose in our lives there exists an omnipresent ever pervasive energy which I call God, but can be called by any other name to describe infinite power, infinite intelligence, infinite love, peace and joy. The Creator of everything. Not a white bearded man in the sky, rather an energy that is pure and non influenceable by any of us. An energy whose principles and laws governing our existence are perfect structures that are both stable and knowable... like the Law of Gravity.

There is no favoritism or discrimination within the Laws of the Universe that govern our experiences and we wouldn't want it any other way. We need to be able to rely on solid structures that don't resemble the flaws of the human condition. Yet it's not an impersonal energy either. We find connection and perfect guidance when we tap into this wondrous energy system with our Creator and of our Creator.

When we become more aware of this intricate energy system, we can learn to abide by and appreciate the underlying perfection that rules our world. It is now scientifically proven, understood and accepted that everyone and everything is ultimately made of energy, including our thoughts. Every thought we have is transmitted into the energetic network of invisible communication so powerfully that it's literally creating our reality and projecting its imagery onto the movie screens of our lives. We are completely in control of all of it and we are just beginning to understand how powerful we are as the creator and director of our lives.

In many ways, we have to unlearn what we know to be true, and this can be a grueling process because we have to throw away blame for anything that's either happened in the past or that is missing in the present. We have to come to terms with the fact that there is nothing outside of us that can stop us from living the life we came to live.

The truth is, we were born having everything we need for this journey. This is a RELEARN since we were taught from an early age that we have to go out and make something of our lives instead of simply being our authentic unique selves and following our intuition and permit the natural unfolding of our lives. To row our boats gently down the stream, which puts us in the flow of nature's rhythm. This requires a consciousness that has faith in the stream of life and its source. A willingness to row, but gently, because the stream is doing the majority of the steering and getting us to where we need to go.

It is our consciousness that is delivering our reality and to the degree we are AWARE of the abundance that exists everywhere, we will either be able to experience it or miss the mark completely. The majority of people in the world are stuck in the illusion that they are not good enough somehow at whatever part of their life is in turmoil. The collective consciousness believes the world does not have enough resources for everyone to live happy, healthy lives. Some people in positions of power want to perpetuate this mistruth, out of their own fear that there is not enough to go around for everyone.

The truth is there is enough- food, water, shelter, etc. The external problem is distribution. The internal problem is fear. The true problem lies in the lack of consciousness to solve the problems of the world. Instead we attempt to solve these problems at the level of thinking that created them in the first place and very little progress is made as a result.

Every single person that is on the Earth right now was born with a mission, a part to play. Whether a person is interested in waking up to it or not is an act of free will. For those that are interested it starts with getting in touch with what that mission is and then making the necessary changes within to prepare for it. Developing our souls to awaken to our mission and become more conscious in our lives is underrated. Maybe because it is *really* hard work and most people aren't up for it. Doing the hard work within is necessary to move the collective consciousness closer to peace and prosperity. The world doesn't need changing, the people who live in it do. The world appears chaotic because the majority of people are a mess. It's hard to imagine that if we clean up our own act we can make a difference, but we can… make a difference, which is why every single person needs to start right now.

As Spiritual Beings in a physical body there are many things we can do and participate in that carry the potential for soul development. Mind and heart activities that keep us grounded to the Earth while allowing our spirits to soar are a great start. Hiring a life coach to assist in our soul's development can fast track our success. A consistent practice of prayer and meditation open channels for perfect guidance to flow.

I've had enough of my own life lessons to know that wishful thinking or any other mindset that believes life will just magically workout won't get a person very far. We can't just sit, pray and meditate, and expect things to come to us. It requires action on our part. I watched Oprah's interview with Jim Carrey about the Law of Attraction and he said this, "you can't just visualize... and then go eat a sandwich". I've tried it and it doesn't work:) While visualization is great and involves calling forth specific desires to manifest into reality, we have to take action to bring anything to fruition.

Having knowledge and understanding about the Laws of the Universe are helpful; releasing and surrendering to God's Will in our lives is essential. This takes some work and involves a willingness to lay your burdens down. When the time came for me to lay my burdens down, I was more than ready. Are you ready? If you are...

This is a book about transition... blocks, challenges, a lack of resources, and the Perfect Guidance to overcome and transcend anything that is keeping you from the life you were meant for... and how you can surrender and release all stress, worries, doubts & fears in the process, on your journey to realizing your fullest and highest potential. It's a book about finding anything you feel is missing in your life. As humans, we crave peace, joy and love... we can't help but crave the experience of them. But if you are experiencing a crisis and are in transition, those gifts can seem elusive and may even feel non-existent. Yet, there is always hope knocking at your door. I'm knocking at your door with this book, to share with you my incredible journey of crises and heartbreak and the truths that set me free. The secrets to success are found, here & now, in this book.

I wish you peace, joy and love on your journey, Godspeed! Deborah Naone

INTRODUCTION

For the majority of my life, I misplaced my power. I believed in the illusion that everyone and everything outside of myself could affect and determine my successes and failures. I cared deeply about what others thought which caused me to create experiences for myself that were out of alignment with who I really am.

In Marianne Williamson's book "A Return To Love", there is a powerful passage. "ONLY LOVE IS REAL. God is not the author of fear. You are. So the problem with the world is that we have strayed from God, or wandered away from love. The introduction to A Course in Miracles States:

> Nothing real can be threatened.
> Nothing unreal exists.
> Herein lies the peace of God.

What that means is this:

> Love is real. It's an eternal creation and nothing can destroy it.
> Anything that isn't love is an illusion.
> Remember this, and you'll be at peace.

The opposite of love is fear, but what is all encompassing can have no opposite."

Hence the illusion of any condition, experience or situation that's based in fear. We have all been in a very deep sleep, unaware of the "real world" that God created. It is here. It's always been here. We just can't see it because we aren't conscious enough. It is our universal mission to wake up to it, to develop our consciousness so that we can create the awareness to finally see it. At every turn we are gently nudged to remember our true nature, which is Love. When we are willing to release to our true nature based in love, and surrender to God; we reunite the world and in turn receive its glory.

For me it was so easy to fall prey to illusion. I learned fear from a very young age. I was taught to compete in life and it seemed like there were competitions for everything, whether it be on my swim team, soccer team, tennis team, dance competitions, spelling bees, grades at school or trying to snatch the last cookie from the cookie jar at home, everything was a competition. I became focused on trying to win at all times at all costs, in everything. I looked for ways to stand out through achievement. As a result I learned how to invent different versions of myself, trying on several different masks... not realizing I was already a perfect creation exactly the way I was.

At the age of 13, when my parents got divorced, I became fearful. As a person who tried to win at everything, I lost something BIG that year. My family of 6 was split apart and the loss ran deep. There weren't counselors like there are today so my brother, sisters and I were left to deal with our feelings on our own.

By the time I was a young adult I had learned to navigate the external world fairly well, wearing a shiny coat of armor for protection, never fully healing the fearful parts of me that lay just beneath the surface. On the outside, I was young and outwardly fearless. Inside, I was still a hurt young girl, my wounds fairly undetectable. Life doesn't wait for internal healing. Instead it propels us forward working with the level of consciousness it finds. My method of operation was to set aside any hurt feelings and focus solely on getting an education, winning in business and earning money to buy things that would make me feel better.

Deep into my 4th year of college, in an upper division marketing class, my grade solely depended on creating a business plan from scratch. I was required to go through the process of trying to lease retail space for the full experience of business plan immersion. I got so into it that I decided then and there I would start the business 'for real'. I shared the idea with my Dad and he promptly told me to set up 3 meetings with banks to get funding and agreed to go along for support. I proceeded to pitch my business to 3 different bankers who all had the same response that went something like, "I am impressed with your presentation and like your enthusiasm. It sounds like a good idea but the statistic for small businesses that fail is close to 90% and we can't take that risk. Come back and see me when you have your first year's track record under your belt and I'll be able to you..."

What I didn't know then, was that my Dad already knew this would be the outcome. He wanted to test my commitment, enthusiasm and tolerance for rejection. Apparently I passed the test that day as he had already thought of another way to fund the business. He steered me to sell stock in which he would be willing to be the majority stockholder, with the condition that I sold the balance of stock to others, which I did. My business venture was off the ground and fully funded within a short period of time.

From the beginning, and for the duration of the business, I did not entertain one single thought that there was even a remote possibility that I could fail or that my business could fail, therefore it didn't. It was very successful right out of the gate. Five years later I put the business up for sale with a business broker when I had become engaged to be married. My business broker looked at the books and within 2 weeks announced she had a buyer. My business broker herself had fallen in love with the documented cash flow, left her job and bought my business.

After taking a couple of months off for the wedding and honeymoon, I went to work for a then, Fortune 100 Company in outside Sales. I fast tracked my way to top performance resulting in recognition and winning slots to attend several achievement conferences. At that time, I didn't notice the personal power that was slowly leaking from me to my employer. It's like a ghost in the night that comes and steals a little bit of joy to begin preparations for the next chapter in our lives. I ignored those small gentle nudges that suggested I was better suited as an entrepreneur to unleash my full creativity. Some time around the 4th or 5th year the gentle nudges became stronger and I realized that I was working solely for the paycheck. My passion and purpose became diluted beyond recognition. Eventually I quit, and after a couple of other short stints, I bounced into commercial real estate development- swinging for the fences during a boom market. I was looking to make more than enough money and in the process buy myself time to figure out my life's direction.

I never questioned whether or not there was a higher power, a higher truth, and a perfect process that created everyone and everything in existence. Maybe I was blessed in this way, to have at least a small foundation of "knowingness" about this ever-pervasive perfect presence that permeates all of creation.

My studies over the years would lead me to ever-greater understanding. But still, even with this information, peace, sustainable prosperity and true abundance eluded me. Even the meaning and purpose of my life eluded me and I was left with questions that I had no answers to. I had a feeling in my body that ran deep and jagged piercing my heart, I knew something was missing but I couldn't put my finger on it. My intuition was telling me things weren't right at home either and as it turned out, I was right. My marriage ended in divorce and I became a single working mom at the age of 32 raising my 2 sons who were then 5 and 7; taking on the role of the primary support both physically and financially.

Intuitively I knew I was meant to do something great in the area of my work (we all are) but I had no idea what it was. The area of my life that was deeply fulfilling was parenting my 2 boys, and it would ultimately become my greatest joy through the years and my biggest achievement. Meanwhile, I continued to work in commercial real estate development, made good money, and settled into success without purpose nicely. The people I worked with brought joy in many ways but I was faced with the fact that I had made a decision once again to barter my talents and gifts for a paycheck in an exchange that helped others become wealthy. Anytime I entertained the idea of breaking free, I was haunted. I had been given the golden handcuffs of a 6-figure base salary, every perk imaginable plus the opportunity to earn bonuses off my leasing efforts in the developments I worked on and I had been with the company for 9 years. So anytime I thought of an idea to work for myself again as an entrepreneur I reminded myself I was a single parent with enormous responsibilities financially. I called on the banker ghosts of the past to remind me of statistics, and this time I believed them.

I understood the concept of listening to my Internal Guidance System, but I couldn't find a way to tap into it with confidence. I understood the concept that our thoughts create our reality, but I couldn't control the negative and resistant thoughts keeping me from manifesting a better path. I understood human energy analysis but hard as I tried I couldn't seem to positively affect my 3rd chakra that has to do with personal power. I felt alone in all of it and continued to make employers and situations my 'source' for financial security in the world. I was caught in space and time and I was... WAY OFF COURSE.

Something really strange happens when we aren't willing to make the necessary changes to proactively change course, we lose control of the rocket ship and it inevitably crashes. Therefore, in a way that only Spirit can, when all attempts to intercede failed, my rocket ship spun out of control and crashed. I was pulled from the wreckage and brought to my knees, my rocket ship in a billion small pieces. What I didn't realize at the time is there would be no possibility for a rebuild of the same ship, for that ship and navigation no longer served me. The new rocket ship would need to be built in the likeness of its original design (without my inventions or modifications), one that included my fullest and highest potential; the promise I was born with.

To kick the process off, everything that needed to fall away... did. The commercial real estate market crashed in 2009. With the security of my 6-figure base salary and a bonus of $97,000 on the line, I was getting internal messages it was time to go but I was too afraid to quit. I had a mortgage, bills to pay and 2 sons to provide for. I was experiencing the same set of crises that many people faced during this difficult time. And like so many others, the winds of change were upon me. I found myself in situations at work that would make most people quit. There was a small problem though, if I was to quit, per my contract, I would forgo the $97,000 bonus... and I really needed that bonus for security. I tried to hold on in some ways but in a subconscious way through my actions I was sending off a very blatant smoke signal asking to be fired. Then, when I wasn't strong enough to make the choice on my own to quit, choice was abdicated for me, and I got fired. The irony is... I never was paid the $97,000 that was owed me.

How it played out for me felt cruel at the time. I proceeded to lose every material thing I had identified so strongly with... identified with who I was as a person...and what I was worth. Several months after I had been fired I was driving home to my beautiful house in an upscale neighborhood. As I rounded the corner and looked at my home there were more than 40 large black birds covering my front lawn and the roof of my house- with no source of food or anything drawing them in. I looked around at all of my neighbor's houses and there wasn't one single bird to be found. I got a chill up my spine. I knew then, there was more change coming my way, and this was a sign.

Around 5 months later, I lost my house to foreclosure. It was a very unsettling time in our lives and the price to pay emotionally ran deeper than the inability to make the mortgage payment. The day I drove away for the very last time, I heard a then small voice whisper, "If God can take it all away, He can give it all back too and MORE, when you're ready..."

My faith was tested over and over again and in ever increasing ways. I lived with an average bank account balance under $100 for years. I must have been testing whether or not God, my Angels and the Universe would keep me safe (and I was... kept safe).

I went to work for a medical company and then a technology company that paid what felt like "criminal" wages at the time in comparison to what I was accustomed to earning. I tried to start over but it became clear early in the process that my earnings would be capped at half of what my income was in the past. I considered it a factor of the economy but it was really a factor of my mind. I had lost my edge. My confidence was shattered. I tried a number of small business ideas but this time I allowed the potential for failure to enter my thoughts... so nothing ever really got off the ground. I had completely lost faith in myself and in the ability to trust my business instincts.

By this time I had experienced nearly all of the major crises one can go through: financial crisis, relationship crisis, purpose crisis and the one that brought me to my knees, a faith crisis. I never did turn to alcohol or drugs or any addictive remedies. I considered it a luxury to "check out" of life. I had the responsibility of my boys so I didn't have time to consider any options that took me away from those routines and responsibilities. At the time, I didn't have the knowledge to release and surrender because I didn't know what I would be surrendering to. I was so busy making God my co-pilot rather than my pilot, believing that I single-handedly needed to figure everything out on my own. All the while praying to my higher power to "please help me". It didn't occur to me that God with infinite power, infinite wisdom, infinite love, just might make a better pilot than co-pilot!

When I look back on my life I realize how unconscious I was in choosing to not listen and trust in myself. I tuned out the most perfect and powerful guidance, the Internal Guidance System I was born with. I accomplished this by immediately cutting off any emotion that I thought might cause me to feel pain. The problem with that was by stuffing those emotions and feelings it caused an ever greater negative "hit" to my system. If I had been more conscious when those emotions and feelings arrived I would have heard a voice shouting at me, "I will continue to bring you the same experiences over and over until you acknowledge me!"

As a result of my unconsciousness, the School of Hard Knocks became my education system and a familiar playground to get hurt on, time and time again. I even became accustomed to its rules and risks and felt somewhat comfortable earning my Masters there. Eventually, over time, I grew tired of re-enacting the same experiences in different costumes. We all know the definition of insanity as doing the same thing over and over again expecting a different result. When I didn't get the results I was looking for I became increasingly aware of a need to do things differently.

As I became more conscious, I recognized a pattern or rather stages of awareness shifts that had occurred in me: In the early days of earning a living I was creating unconsciously (externally focused). Material possessions and status were the measurement of my success. As a result of worshipping the wrong things I started to feel pain unconsciously (unhappiness in my career, personal relationships, negative thoughts and discontent). CRISES struck! As I became more aware of my misguided pursuits coupled with the need to make big changes in my life and myself, I moved into feeling pain consciously. This was a turning point... that some people refer to as "the Dark Night of the Soul".

I think it is more accurate to call it "the Dark Night of the Ego". It is a moment in time when you are called to remember who you really are and why you came... and to firmly stand in your power with those truths. Now THAT is a really dark night for the Ego, for if you accept the calling, the Ego faces losing tremendous power. THIS IS THE TIME TO RELEASE & SURRENDER. Your true identity will prevail, and you will have achieved one of Mankind's greatest victories… to overcome the illusions of the world. It is only in this state of mind that you can create consciously and enjoy the fruits of true abundance. We are meant to enjoy material things, and we can experience the richness of them at their highest levels when they are created consciously.

STAGES OF AWARENESS:

Unconsciously Create: Identified strongly with and attached to the material world. Fear of losing identity if something falls away such as your- career, money or possessions.

Unconscious Pain: Completely unaware that the pain is a result of creating unconsciously. Strong discontent and possible dis--ease.

Conscious Pain: Aware of the pain associated with creating unconsciously. Signal received that it is time to change.

Consciously Create: Non--identified and Unattached to the temporary material world. Grateful for the experience of material things and feeling free to enjoy them without fear of loss.

HEAVEN
Creating Consciously

STAGES
Conscious Pain

OF
Unconscious Pain

LEARNING A LESSON
Creating Unconsciously
EARTH

Even if you have experienced extreme outward success, if it was achieved by creating unconsciously you will experience both a purpose crisis and a faith crisis. You might be surrounded by all the material possessions you ever dreamed of but if you are unsure about your mission and how to live it daily, you will feel that something is missing in your life, and you'll be right. If you are fearful of anything being taken away from you like your material possessions, a relationship or your job/career, you will eventually be led to experience a crisis in order to transcend the illusion and take back your power.

As you can see from the diagram it is our divine right to experience abundance in our life, including the material possessions we desire. We are here to create and enjoy our manifestations. When we create consciously, we don't release our power to things, for we recognize their temporary nature. Conversely, we appreciate them immensely for what they are and maintain a grateful heart for the experience of them. This is the most fulfilling way to co-exist with the temporary material world. We are spiritual beings having a human experience, we go on, our stuff does not. Our task at hand is to quiet the ego and LEAD with Spirit.

I faced the Dark Night of the Ego and like a typical Libra, I mentally processed it till I understood all its parts...challenging everything I believed. Through the cleansing experience I took the time to face mistruths head on and a raging fire burned inside of me. My old belief system was burnt to ashes. Then, from the ashes, I transitioned and emerged, stronger and with more clarity and peace than I ever imagined. This is the transition that can occur in your life!

CONTENTS

CHAPTER 1
7 BILLION SOULS

The human brain is a powerfully mysterious topic of discussion, especially when contemplating the human condition and how we experience life. Have you ever wondered what God's energy looks like? I have. I've spent 4 decades trying to know the unknowable. But in the deepest recess of my mind I've tried to picture it. I picture an entity of immense energy like a supernova x infinity, not a white bearded man in the sky. Not something outside of us. Quite the opposite, we are inside of it and it is inside of us. And it is EVERYWHERE; there's nowhere it's not.

I imagine inside this immense energy there are infinite galaxies like the cells of our brain. It's infinite because as some galaxies and its parts die off others are born, reborn or renewed. Within one of those galaxies is planet Earth with over 7 billion souls, like 7 billion thoughts, 7 billion divine cells, or rather 7 billion divine sparks of energy. I picture each one of us as Divine Spark or Divine Cell of God's energy. I believe this is what is meant by "we were made in the image and likeness of God". Since everyone and everything is made of energy, it is His energy... and we were created in the likeness of it.

"Every beauty which is seen here below by persons of perception resembles more than anything else that celestial source from which we all came."
-Michelangelo

I suppose anything is possible. If I were God with infinite power, infinite wisdom, and infinite love, what better way to experience life on Earth than to experience it in over 7 billion different ways. A brilliant game to play, one that is layered with more complexities than we can possibly imagine... difficult to imagine given our relative speck of a brain. Yet we have the experience of being powerful creators, and we are. Our imaginations soar with possibilities and we continually push the leading edge of thought higher and higher. We are meaning-making machines. Our entire journey is filled with meaning. Our lives matter. We matter. The energy that we are a part of and that is a part of us, matters. Our Source, from which we are the extension of, makes us more powerful than we can possibly imagine. I imagine there is nothing else like the human experience. We are truly special in that way.

It's unfortunate we have in our experience the illusion of separateness, and that the majority of people on the planet have bought into this illusion. The notion of being separate from each other, from our Source, and from all living things has been engrained in our consciousness. As we continue to evolve our consciousness this myth is destroyed and just like the rocket ship analogy used earlier, the belief shatters to a billion a pieces and truth emerges. We are all connected. We are One collective consciousness experiencing life as Individual expressions of the One life.

God as immense energy, ever pervasive and omnipresent in everyone and everything is the best way to make sense of "Oneness", oneness with God and with every single person and thing that exists on Earth, our "interconnectedness".

"Love the whole world as if it were yourself; then you will truly care for all things."
-Lao Tzu

Are we not continuing to evolve our own consciousness to contribute to the "collective consciousness" so that this will become a recognized universal truth? I believe we are. There is a shift taking place right now that is deepening our understanding, evolving our sensory system and bringing us into alignment with conscious creation. Jesus said, "The Kingdom of Heaven is Within You". It is only when we do the work to improve our inner selves that we begin to see improvements in our outer world. When the "collective consciousness" of people around the globe arrive at this truth and practice it, we will collectively begin to experience Heaven on Earth. But each individual has the power to create it for him or herself right now - when we turn to love as the basis for all of our actions and turn away from the illusions of fear.

For now, we are over 7 billion souls - all connected in this game called Life. Every soul can choose to do the inner work. The world doesn't need changing, the people who live in it do.

"The Lord works from the inside out. The world works from the outside in. The world would take people out of the slums. Christ takes the slums out of people and they take themselves out of the slums. The world would mold men by changing their environment. Christ changes men who then change their environment. The world would change human behaviors but Christ can change human nature."
-Ezra Taft Benson

If you don't think you can make a difference, think again. If you think your life doesn't count, do the math. The laws and principles governing our existence have accounted for every single soul; no soul is apart from the whole. Every soul matters. When you judge, hate or do harm to others, you judge, hate and do harm to yourself and the whole of humanity. When you think war is required, have you not considered that the same resources deployed for war would be better served to work toward peace? War is insane and insanity is as widespread as we will choose to make it. What we give attention to and focus upon grows, it's both principle and law. Our media is completely guilty of playing up fear and keeping people caught in the illusions of the world. They won't change their ways, so each individual must decide whether to support that effort or turn away from it.

As each person turns inward to grow in consciousness, these truths gain greater clarity and focus. Each person contributes to the collective consciousness of the planet with the level of peace that exists in theirself. Peace within creates peace without. Once peace exists in a person, peace is as impenetrable as its source and evil does not exist in such perfection. In fact, evil doesn't exist at all. Listen in on the following conversation between a Professor and a Student...

Does evil exist?

The university professor challenged his students with this question. Did God create everything that exists?

A student bravely replied, "Yes, he did!"

"God created everything? The professor asked.

"Yes sir", the student replied.

The professor answered, "If God created everything, then God created evil since evil exists, and according to the principal that our works define who we are then God is evil".

The student became quiet before such an answer.

The professor was quite pleased with himself and boasted to the students that he had proven once more that the Christian faith was a myth.

Another student raised his hand and said, "Can I ask you a question professor?"

"Of course", replied the professor.

The student stood up and asked, "Professor, does cold exist?"

"What kind of question is this? Of course it exists. Have you never been cold?" The students snickered at the young man's question.

The young man replied, "In fact sir, cold does not exist. According to the laws of physics, what we consider cold is in reality the absence of heat. Every body or object is susceptible to study when it has or transmits energy, and heat is what makes a body or matter have or transmit energy. Absolute zero (--460 degrees F) is the total absence of heat; all matter becomes inert and incapable of reaction at that temperature. Cold does not exist. We have created this word to describe how we feel if we have no heat."

The student continued, "Professor, does darkness exist?"

The professor responded, "Of course it does."

The student replied, "Once again you are wrong sir, darkness does not exist either. Darkness is in reality the absence of light. Light we can study, but not darkness. In fact we can use Newton's prism to break white light into many colors and study the various wavelengths of each color. You cannot measure darkness. A simple ray of light can break into a world of darkness and illuminate it. How can you know how dark a certain space is? You measure the amount of light present. Isn't this correct? Darkness is a term used by man to describe what happens when there is no light present."

Finally the young man asked the professor, "Sir, does evil exist?"

Now uncertain, the professor responded, "Of course as I have already said. We see it every day. It is in the daily example of man's inhumanity to man. It is in the multitude of crime and violence everywhere in the world. These manifestations are nothing else but evil."

To this the student replied, "Evil does not exist sir, or at least it does not exist unto itself. Evil is simply the absence of God. It is just like darkness and cold, a word that man has created to describe the absence of God. God did not create evil. Evil is not like faith or love that exist just as does light and heat. Evil is the result of what happens when man does not have God's love present in his heart. It's like the cold that comes when there is no heat or the darkness that comes when there is no light."

The professor sat down. The young man's name — Albert Einstein.

Evil is a lie we tell ourselves, when we lose all faith in the truth. It is one of the many illusions of the world. When we can overcome these illusions, we will witness world peace. World peace requires our committed practice of the truth and the belief that we are all equal in its pursuit.

"An eye for an eye only ends up making the whole world blind."
-Mahatma Ghandi

And the wisdom from all of the great teachers who have come before us continues to pour into our consciousness like messages in a bottle that will forever float upon the sea... Thich Nhat Hanh wrote in "Living Buddha Living Christ", the following:

"The Kingdom of Heaven may be called the ultimate dimension of reality. When you see only waves, you might miss the water. But if you are mindful, you will be able to touch the water within the wave as well. Once you are capable of touching the water, you will not mind the coming and going of the waves. You are no longer concerned about the birth and death of the wave. You are no longer afraid. You are no longer upset about the beginning or the end of the wave, or that the wave is higher or lower, more or less beautiful. You are capable of letting these ideas go because you have already touched the water."

CHAPTER 2
THE SOUL DEFINED

What is the soul? Soul is a word to describe the central or integral part of something of importance or its vital core. In its most profound sense, it can be described as the 'Essence' of every human being. It is that part of us that is Eternal, Infinite and Universal in truths of the highest. It contains the divine blueprint for our lives and it yearns to express its potential in the fullest way possible.

The concept of the soul is shrouded in mystery, because like God, it can never be fully knowable. Yet we have a sense that it contains our destiny, our dharma. Dr. Wayne Dyer said in his movie, "The Shift" regarding the seed of our soul, something to the effect, If everything in our physical nature was contained in that seed, our hair color, our eye color, and our personality was in there, then it wouldn't be a far stretch to say our purpose was in there too.

The soul is a Sacred place that bridges the spirit realm with the external world, dreams with reality, and collapses the past and future into the present moment - thereby creating the forever Now. And the NOW is the only time we can create anything. The moment we were created we were given Free Will to choose. Free Will to create. Free Will to fail. Free Will to try, try, try again. Free Will to choose to grow in consciousness. Free Will to succeed.

Invictus by William Ernest Henley,

"Out of the night that covers me, Black as the pit from pole to pole, I thank whatever gods may be for my unconquerable soul...

I am the Master of my Fate, I am the Captain of my Soul."

Unconquerable souls, that is what we are. The Will to live- strong. It is from this precious gift that the fountain of miracles pours. When we witness miracles, we are inspired to believe. When we are the recipients of them, we inspire others to believe. When we are born and when we leave the Earth, it's easy to believe. It's in the "in between" we must develop our faith. We must not sit and wait for miracles; we must participate in the creation of them.

In fact, you alone are a miracle. There is no other soul like you. Each soul comes to the Earth with unique gifts. Your unique gifts are so important, so precious in fact, they are meant to play a very specific "role" in the grand scheme of life. Whatever's missing in the perfect puzzle of humanity, you're that piece! Without you, the other pieces can only have relative success in the completion of the puzzle. But here's the real rub. At birth we are required to drink from the "river of forgetfulness", so that it would be in the unfolding of our lives' experiences, with perfect guidance from our Internal Guidance Systems, that we would come to remember who we are and why we came.

You can get very clear about exactly what your gifts are and how you can serve with them and while there may be several "right" paths based on the choices you make, you will find yourself on a right path. How will you know? You will be filled with so much passion and joy you will be overflowing with enthusiasm! You will feel compelled and propelled to share with as many people and in as many ways as you can, your unique gifts and contributions.

You won't be alone in the discovery of your destiny, your dharma; you have support from unseen forces. The process naturally starts when you can no longer face another day without purpose. I know this feeling well, and you may too... so the very first thing to do is breathe. Take in a conscious breath- breathing in... support, breathing out... your worries, doubts and fears.

You're about to discover what breathes you.

CHAPTER 3
THE FORCE BEHIND YOUR BREATH

It was your first breath that announced your arrival, and it's your last breath that signals your departure. All of the breaths in between facilitate the creation of your life's story. Our breath IS that important. We don't think about breathing though, we just do it. We unconsciously take each breath with absolute confidence that this whole breathing thing will just take care of itself, and it does.

Conscious breathing is experienced in different ways. For example, we all have something that we love to do, that we were born to do, and that we are passionate about. For some it is the participation in an individual sport like golf or tennis, for others a group sport, or simply a routine of going for a run or walk each day or surfing the perfect wave. There is also music and art, performing and acting, and countless other ways to express one's self. These passions don't just show up unintentionally, they are very meaningful, for they are deeply embedded in the seed of your soul and desire to be experienced and expressed. So whether you recognized your passion from an early age or discovered it more recently, if you pay close attention, you will find a force present while experiencing your passion. Your awareness sharpens and you enter what is referred to as "the zone" and when this happens your awareness zeros in on one thing... conscious breathing.

People talk about "getting in the zone" when they are sharply focused in their passion. That zone is the harnessing of energy coming through you from Source energy and it's intuitively connected to a deep place within. It is the place where we subliminally sense the presence of God (or any other source you call by name), even if we are not fully aware of it. It is the place where Spirit is made visible and our souls are made visible- by giving us a glimpse of our potential and the possibility of our greatest achievements.

You've experienced it... there you are playing full out in your passion and suddenly the world outside goes quiet, everything around you seemingly disappears. Time collapses, there is only the present moment. Your focus - intense - and you feel completely in the zone. Think Matt Damon in the movie "Bagger Vance" or Kevin Costner in "The Perfect Game". When you reach this state of mind the only sound is the sound of your breath. It both calms and excites. It takes over any thinking and propels you into just being. You feel at one with a powerful energy that gives you the sensation of pure bliss. With each breath you feel deeply alive and fully present. Nothing can enter-; negative thoughts and feelings aren't even possible in this moment. You have found it... whatever it is that you've searched long and hard for... this is it! This is what it means to be in the zone. This is what it means to be consciously breathing.

It has been said that God is happiest when His children are at play. The sound of your breath is like hearing the word "Yes" being echoed. You just want to freeze the moment, the feeling, the perfection of it all. If you could bottle it and sell it you'd be a billionaire. But you can't and won't ever be able to because it doesn't belong to you. It is not coming from Man, it cannot be manufactured by Man, and it cannot be contained by Man. God is the force behind each breath. This is the love of God for his creation. This is the energy of God experiencing life on Earth through us. God is as close as our breath...God breathes us.

Another example of experiencing our breath is through concentrated forms of breathing techniques and commitment to connection made available through Prayer, Meditation, and countless forms of exercise such as Yoga, Martial Arts and Dance, to name just a few. Medical research and scientific studies have concluded that there are enormous benefits to our "whole being" associated with these activities.

Conscious breathing moves you into a heightened state of consciousness, opening the channels of higher frequencies- allowing the highest connection and messaging to occur. It establishes a "state of wellbeing" by reducing the stress hormone cortisol while simultaneously increasing oxytocin, which is known as "the feel good hormone". Conscious breathing has also been strongly associated with Emotional Intelligence. Breathing has the power to calm any storm and neuroscience has proven this:

"Very recent research shows that the oscillations connected to the rate of breathing are very tied to bringing sensory data together as perceptions. In fact, breathing is highly connected to altering perceptions related to emotions and different physical activities. Breathing exercises are well known to alter perceptions including helping change fear to relaxation. Synchronous brain waves between regions related to breathing and mental experience may be a mechanism whereby self-observation and breathing exercises alter perceptions in meditation."
-Dr. Jon Lieff, MD

Now, breathe deep into the present moment. Are you ready to transform your hardships? If you feel blocked, if your heart is broken, if your situation feels hopeless, just take 6 deep breaths. Notice that you don't breathe alone. Something far greater than yourself is in the essence of your breath. God is right there with you. Every day take a moment to acknowledge your breath and its source. You will feel a sensation of being acknowledged back. To be conscious of your breath is to be conscious of life itself. Never taking one single breath for granted.

CHAPTER 4
CONSCIOUSNESS

The basic definition of consciousness is the state of being awake and aware of one's surroundings, a person's mind and thoughts.

"Humanity's finest minds have from ancient times sought the answer to one of the greatest mysteries of existence. What is the nature of man's spiritual world? All the forces of reason—science, philosophy, art, literature—have combined in the effort to cast light on this mysterious realm known as consciousness. Human beings possess the most wonderful of all gifts—reason with its keen insight into the remote past and the future, its penetration into the sphere of the unknown, its world of dreams and fantasy, creative solutions to practical and theoretical problems and the realization of the most daring plans."
-A. Spirkin Dialectical Materialism

One way to experience varying degrees of consciousness (in its simplicity) is by having you go for a walk with me in nature. As we begin to stroll through a beautiful park filled with trees, plants, flowers and wildlife- you first begin to see and experience everything in black and white, unaware of the beauty that surrounds you. Then slowly, as your awareness grows, the view starts to fill in with some color and you make a point to look around a little more than you did before. Then, by focusing your attention sharply, you see vibrant colors and textures of every variety. Excitement fills the air. Then, as if you are being rewarded (and you are) you suddenly become aware of every perfect detail in the trees, plants, flowers, birds and rabbits that surround you in this abundant environment. Colorful butterflies grace your presence and gratitude for the experience fills your heart. And then, as if you willed it (and you have) your sensory system is bombarded with pleasure, pure bliss, as you witness God's perfection in this perfect moment and you silently say, "Thank you God, thank you for my life."

"The moment one gives close attention to anything, even a blade of grass, it becomes a mysterious, awesome, indescribably magnificent world in itself."
-Henry Miller

When you reach that stage of awareness and consciousness, energetically speaking, you are vibrating at a high level and affecting the quantum field of consciousness in a very positive way. You are signaling to the Universe that you trust in its infinite power to provide for you experiences that you both want and desire. To which the Universe nods back and orchestrates to give you more; it's Law. When you consciously come into alignment vibrationally and are congruent with the object of your desire - you will see it manifest in your reality. It's an inside-out-attraction-push, not an outside-in-attraction-pull.

These manifestations are what we live for and when accompanied by peace, joy and love, there is nothing more exhilarating than experiencing the feeling of having everything, even if for only a moment in time. One moment in time provides a deep satisfaction that can be followed by more moments in time.

I wrote an article called "What it Means to be Conscious". Here's what it said...

The awake person is not at odds with the world. He is at peace and practices, "allowing" by releasing himself from both outcomes and expectations. He surrenders to "what is" and is deeply in the flow of nature's rhythm. He is "in the world but not of it", as he acknowledges the connectedness of the earthly and eternal realm. He is the observer of it all, but he is also a participant. He knows many people are suffering in the world unaware of their own suffering, so he is compassionate and does what he can to help others. He lives fluidly, instead of being reactionary and responding to the world based on unconscious rules, beliefs, fears and limitations. He is able to consciously evaluate each situation in the moment and instinctively know exactly what to do and how to respond in order to gain the most resourceful outcome for all involved. He lives with intent and has a spiritual practice to seek his highest truth, greatest good, and purest thoughts so that he may serve humanity with joy and love during his time on Earth.

I believe this to be the pursuit for higher consciousness as we continually push through to ever-new heights and gain greater insight about our true nature. It would be very rare indeed to personally know someone who is "fully conscious" as in "Christ consciousness" and I personally haven't had the honor to know someone who is but that doesn't mean that they don't exist or it's not possible. The focus here is the pursuit and progression of higher consciousness. And if there is anything within us blocking, slowing down or stopping us from forward progression we will be required to do the "inner game" work. Sometimes this means transcending our deepest fears to greet our greatest desires. Sometimes it means it's time to change.

CHAPTER 5
TRANSITION - TIME TO CHANGE

At the center of any transition is a hurricane in the form of a Crisis. The most prevalent crises are the following: Relationship, Financial, Health, Purpose and the one they all have in common is the one that has the power to take you to your knees, a Faith crisis.

Has a crisis or series of crises brought you to your knees? Have you felt like God hasn't heard your prayers? If you are down on your knees, you probably are also feeling a bit relieved since the very act of releasing and surrendering is an opportunity to lay your burdens down and hand them over to a higher power. The weight of the problem too heavy to carry on your shoulders another day.

At some point in every person's life, a crisis or a series of crises will serve as a catalyst for change. No one is spared of this universal experience. So common and yet so deeply personal that when a person is going through such a crisis they feel like they're the only one. This feeling is perfectly normal, in fact it's textbook.

Every single one of us becomes the eye of the storm when the need for change is required and where a transition becomes the only way to move forward and grow. Transitions are a complete disruption to life as we know it and it's normal to feel lost and alone during one. The hardest part about losing our way, is finding our way back... It takes courage and commitment and most importantly, a huge leap of faith.

Are you in crisis? If you are, you are EXACTLY where you are supposed to be right now. This will sound strange to you, but a crisis signals you are GROWING in consciousness. For on the other side of this crisis you will have a breakthrough that will remove all previous blocks, allowing you to flow once again in the direction of your dreams.

To get to the other side requires that you do 2 things, release & surrender. Releasing your troubles, worries, doubts & fears clears a path for perfect guidance to reach you. Einstein said, "No problem can be solved from the same level of consciousness that created it." We must transcend the problem to find the solution and that requires releasing and accepting it for what it is and honoring it for the lesson it brings, then it can be transcended. Surrendering doesn't mean giving up, it's a way of taking responsibility for your life, for it strips you of all masks and allows your authentic self to surface. When you are operating in authenticity, you become what I call "unstoppable grace".

So the day has come. The winds of change are upon you. It's time to make a decision. Stay the same or change. If you have experienced a repetitive pattern of the same lesson showing up in different costumes, you will be ready to commit to change. The alternative will be far too painful to endure. So now is the time to grasp one of the most important Laws, the Law of Cause and Effect.

Nothing happens by chance or outside this universal law. Every action has a compatible reaction or consequence as in "We reap what we sow". The most important lesson involving human conduct is seen in the Cosmic Law of Cause and Effect with every action having an equal and opposite reaction. Every human thought, word and deed is a Cause that sets off a wave of energy throughout the universe which in turn creates the Effect- whether we like it or not. The law is impartial it simply operates. As a result, our Free Will to choose can either bring us joy or pain.

You are squarely at the center of choice, with Free Will to choose anything you want to Be, Have or Do. If you don't like what you have chosen, then you and only you have the power to choose again. If you've chosen negligently, only you have the power to turn things around through right action. Right action causes Right effect. It doesn't work to simply pray to God to fix something.

I once listened to Derek Rydall, Author of "Emergence- Seven Steps for Radical Life Change", and on one of his podcasts he said something to the effect- "Are you down on your knees looking up and praying for God to fix something? Because if you are, He's looking back at you saying- that's what I have you for". I had an aha moment... that solidified for me what it is to take full responsibility for our lives. That God doesn't magically fix things - we have to ask for guidance and then take right action to fix whatever it is that needs fixing. To ultimately learn to make better choices at every turn by tuning into internal guidance.

If you have been feeling stuck, blocked and unsure about what to do next, you're either squarely in the middle of a crisis or being set up for one. This can be a very trying time. You are on your own to ultimately transcend it. There is a line in the movie "P.S. I Love You" that I have never forgotten. "So now, all alone or not you gotta walk ahead. Thing to remember is... if we're all alone, then we're all together in that too." Let that line and its power bring you comfort. As I said before, no one is spared of crises in life, so we're all together in that too.

Are you willing to say "Yes" to your divine calling that is waiting on the other side of your crises? Saying "Yes" to these questions means committing to your "Yes". It won't be easy to transcend and transition. It will take hard work. You WILL feel like giving up at some point in the process, and you mustn't. You will release powerful emotions that have been trapped or suppressed and it won't feel good in the moments leading up to the release. You will be challenged over and over to release & surrender and you won't fully understand what is being asked of you at times, but you must keep striving to understand and you will, eventually, understand.

This I can assure you, if you can hold the course and stay true to yourself while releasing what no longer serves you and surrendering to a force that created our world and everything in it, you will reach the inevitable success of pure and absolute freedom. And you will be happier than you ever imagined. And better yet, it will be sustainable happiness. The good news...Once you break through to a new level of consciousness, there is no return. You can look forward to a time in your life when the tests and lessons become less and less, fewer and farther between.

CHAPTER 6
CHALLENGE TO FREEDOM

If you are in a good place in your life, and you feel that you have worked long and hard at being successful, I have a different question for you. Are you truly Free?

Do you experience total freedom in your life? Are you free to make any choice that inspires you? If not, what binds you? What do you need to release and surrender to? Who might you need to become consciously to become totally free? Those of you that find yourselves reading this chapter, you may have been contemplating freedom at a deep level. Your soul may be longing for freedom, and crying out for purpose.

There will always be challenges to freedom in the form of expectations:

1. Expectations of others, especially the people in your inner circle
2. Expectations of groups or friendship circles
3. Expectations at work or that come from work
4. Expectations of society

It all comes down to values. When you take the time to order your value system, you have the best approach available to combat any freedom challenge that presents itself. Every person has the right to choose for themselves the ordering of their values.

One example of ordering a value system looks like this. I make my decisions in the following order:

1. God
2. My Health (SQ, EQ, PQ, IQ)
3. My Family
4. My Creed - Love, Give, Laugh, Explore & Experience

In this example, when I have made a choice to do something and I am challenged with the freedom to do it, my first lens is God. If in fact it's a choice that is directly associated with my mission in life I will give the appropriate response to the challenge and forge ahead. I will feel solid in my decision knowing that it honors God and the commitment I have made to myself.

Throughout our lives we are continuously working on the 4 Q's:
SQ (Spiritual Intelligence)
EQ (Emotional Intelligence)
PQ (Physical Intelligence)
IQ (Intelligence Quotient).

We are a house with 4 rooms and each should be attended to. We must design a life to spend time in each room; otherwise the investment will have been lost on us.

Balance is one of the key principles of life. Allow yourself these treasures...

-A Daily Practice / Know Thyself -
-A Spiritual Retreat
-Time in Nature -
-Time at Play
-Time to Learn Something New

It is our responsibility in the highest to find ways to relax, enjoy, learn and grow.

I believe that when we understand that every moment and every experience has been chosen by us for the gift that it contains, and when we choose to accept and embrace that gift, we are well on our way to becoming the conscious creators of our lives. We are on our way toward mastering the principles and laws that govern our existence. This is where true freedom lies.

We are freedom fighters, each and every one of us. We may all have different ideas about what an ideal life looks like, but the common denominator is our desire for freedom. It is our inherent nature to want to be free to choose, free to express and free to create. As Americans, if we want it for ourselves we must also want it for others, without exception.

Our perceptions, by their very nature are flawed. Valuing appearances can be a fatal flaw. I believe appearances are in fact illusions in the world and it is part of our mission in becoming more conscious to overcome the illusions of the world. After all the truth, stripped naked from all appearances, reveals that we all come from the same place. A world without borders or barriers to freedom where all people are free to consciously create and live in peace- is a noble and worthwhile pursuit.

CHAPTER 7
PURPOSE AND GUIDANCE

How and when does someone arrive at a point in their life when the topic of PURPOSE becomes the most important thing to contemplate? How often does the subject of purpose as it relates to one's life purpose surface at the dinner table? Why is the topic uncomfortable to discuss for most... and if someone isn't sure of their own purpose, why is it so elusive?

For starters, there is a false state of being created by the ego. The ego wants you to identify strongly with the physical world so much so that your identity becomes tied to who you are is what you do and what your worth is what you have and the size of your bank account. Dr. Wayne Dyer referred to the EGO in the movie "The Shift" as an acronym to mean -Edge God Out, which is exactly what the ego tries to do falsely leading you to believe that you are all alone in this dog eat dog world. The ego's motto is "Every Man for Himself" and we're taught to compete with others for everything we want.

An awakening to purpose doesn't happen through logical or predictable sequences or timing. It doesn't discriminate based on age, gender, nationality, education or economic status. Your family members, close friends and co-workers don't awake to their own purpose at the same time you awake to yours, thus creating the illusion of separateness. At any given point in time family members and friends, the very people we love and care about, seem to be on a different stair on the staircase to awakening. To further confuse the issue we have no way of knowing which stair they are on or at what pace they are climbing.

Purpose in the context of our lives has several delicious layers. I believe the #1 purpose for all of humanity is to awaken to our true identity; a divine spark of God's loving energy. To ultimately remember we're rooted in love and all of our actions should come from love. That fear is an illusion in the dream of all people still asleep. We will see the real world, whole and perfect, when we shift our consciousness to truth thereby dispelling the illusions and overcoming false reality. When all people participate in this awareness we will finally be able to witness Heaven on Earth.

Our purpose also contains Universal as well as Individual pursuits. For example, a Universal purpose is to serve your fellow Man and be of service to humanity. Your Individual purpose may be to lend your voice to a cause such as "No child shall go hungry" or it may be to win a Grammy or the Nobel Peace Prize. It may be to raise the child that goes on to win an Oscar or become the next President. It may be to love your family, model that love within a community and the world at large. It could be to provide joy to children as a coach or the owner of an ice cream shop. It could be to help others realize their dreams or contribute to raising the consciousness of the planet. Your purpose for working on an important project could be to stay in the moment and give your full attention to it. Whatever it is from the most monumental to the minute; it came with you into this life.

You don't have to go out and try to find it. Everything you're destined for, including Universal and Individual purpose is contained in the seed of your soul. There is perfect guidance available to you- if you'll choose to make it welcome. If you'll allow it to surface. If you'll choose to listen to it. If you'll choose to act on it and become it.

We were never meant to be lost while experiencing life on Earth. We were born with a compass and a promise that we would always have help from the unseen dimension. This compass came in the form of an Internal Guidance System; its workings straightforward. For every choice we make we either feel good, neutral or bad. If we make a choice and we feel good to the core of our being, we've made a good choice. If we feel neutral, it's a choice whose consequence won't have a major impact one way or the other. If we feel bad, we have chosen something that was out of alignment with our soul. IT IS really that simple. Pay attention to how you FEEL at all times.

If you make a choice that causes you to feel bad, the best path would be to make an immediate correction, apologize if another is involved, and choose again. Your job is to feel good as much and as often as possible. Your job is to allow yourself to FEEL everything. Your Internal Guidance System can't function at its highest level unless you allow yourself to feel. Once a choice has been made it is then sent off to be FELT. When you allow the process to work for you will know when you've made good choices or not. And it's ok to make mistakes from time to time because once you have chosen something that makes you feel bad you'll be signaled to Stop, Redirect, and Choose again.

If you don't allow yourself to feel because you are trying to protect yourself on some level from the pain it might bring -then you have diverted your perfect guidance system, and you will experience the effect of your choice in a different way. The diversion wreaks havoc by bringing you more opportunities to FEEL this feeling. If you continue to block this feeling more of the same experiences in different costumes will continue to show up until you let it in and let it process properly through your Internal Guidance System. Once processed correctly, the feeling will dissipate.

Your value system will create the framework necessary for guidance to flow effortlessly. Know thyself! Know your values. Know what you stand for. The more you align your head with your heart, the more easily you will feel 'in a nano second' whether something feels right or wrong. This realization has enormous impact on your life, on your relationships and on your outcomes.

"Self-realization means that we have been consciously connected with our Source of being. Once we have made this connection, then nothing can go wrong..." -Swami Paramananda

In the 7 Habits of Highly Effective People, Stephen Covey described a center, a lens through which we see the world, where our vision & values reside.

"Whatever is at the center of our life will be the source of our security, guidance, wisdom & power. These 4 factors - Security, Guidance, Wisdom, and Power are interdependent. Security and clear guidance bring true wisdom, and wisdom becomes the spark or catalyst to release and direct power. When these four factors are present together, harmonized and enlivened by each other, they create a the great force of a noble personality, a balanced character, a beautifully integrated individual."

Stephen Covey calls the center principles. But then... On Page 319 at the end of his book, a nice surprise is found in the form of a note. He goes on to write-

"A Personal Note - As I conclude this book, I would like to share my own personal conviction concerning what I believe to be the source of correct principles. I believe that correct principles are natural laws, and that God, the Creator and Father of us all is the source of them, and also the source of our conscience... To the degree to which we align ourselves with correct principles, divine endowments will be released within our nature enabling us to fulfill the measure of our creation."

It is a perfect system. God's laws and principles operating in the external world and God's guidance operating in each one of us directing our purpose through our Internal Guidance System.

CHAPTER 8
PERMISSION

Permission has the power to move you forward or hold you back. Permission is tied to having the freedom to make your choices and freedom is tied to the truths you believe in. One of the most repeated quotes in the history of Mankind is, "The truth will set you free". Based on that, let me ask you the following questions: Whose truth will you live by? Whose wisdom and guidance hold the most value for you and that you listen to first above anyone else? Whose permission are you waiting for? These are huge questions- so I want to flag them as such. The fact is, the answers to these questions may have caused you to remain stuck for years and for some of you, the majority of your life.

You may have listened to and believed in another person's truth and invested largely in that belief or set of beliefs about how the world works. It could have been a parent, a teacher, a spouse, an older sibling, a best friend... the list goes on and on. Sometimes we resonate strongly to certain beliefs of others and so when we hear them we recognize them as truth and this is good! Other times we aren't so sure... and in our uncertainty we take the lazy route and just believe for the sake of believing, because we haven't dialed in on our own belief about something.

What if on occasion someone close to you was there by perfect design to try and influence your belief about something- only for the purpose of you to challenge it so that you could strengthen your own core belief and stand in your own truth. After all, the people closest to us have contracted to help us learn our lessons before we entered this earthly realm so why not help us with this one, even if they aren't consciously aware of their role? Have you ever thought of it that way?

If we were designed to take on another's belief system then the most dominant person would prevail and we would eventually see a bunch of robots walking around. Unfortunately, we do see this in society and when the vast majority of people are stuck in survival mode, this is at the base of what's really going on. They have forsaken their power, their truth and their beliefs for someone else's ideas of how the world operates.

There is no one that has more authority over your life than you. Only you can determine what is right for you. Unless you are under the age of 18 (for safety reasons), there is no one's permission you must seek to fulfill your life's calling. When you make the decision to yield to God's purpose, the blocks diminish and a powerful energy begins to flow through you, as you.

You begin to experience the fullness of your being and your external reality begins to shift in unimaginable ways... painting a picture of an abundant world where nothing is lacking and there is enough to go around for everyone. There is nothing to fight for.

You are always in charge of how little or how grand your life experiences are. This is not a permission-based process. When you acknowledge that you are the creator of your life with divine guidance, you are no longer a victim, even if experiences in life have brought you trauma. Whatever healing is required will always be in motion to set you free. When you are willing to learn and grow and accept the past for its purpose to develop your soul, you will experience a quantum leap in consciousness.

Gaining in consciousness means saying "yes" to your Yes (mission in life). I personally remained stuck for quite awhile. I kept waiting for signs outside of myself to validate my next step, my next move, and my choices regarding my future. I knew intuitively that I was divinely inspired to pursue a certain direction in my life, but I would hesitate to act on that guidance. I did a lot to procrastinate the very things that would move me forward. I got very good at listening to my Internal Guidance System - but I became frozen in action when I received the green light. Then during my daily practice, I heard a voice, "whose permission are you waiting for?" I about fell out of my seat. From that moment on, I made a decision to walk confidently in the direction of my dream and not allow anyone to derail me.

You may experience several people close to you trying to derail you. Don't let it upset you. They are doing you a huge favor by allowing you to practice out loud why you won't be budged and why you refuse to give up. This interaction creates an even greater momentum and solidifies the commitment you've made to yourself and to God. Once I solved this one, I vowed to take decisive action to live into my dream. You've heard the phrase, "you don't need to see the whole staircase, you just need to take the next step" and it's true. You will be guided every step of the way, but you must take those steps. God won't do the walking for you, that's what you're here for.

CHAPTER 9
CREATING REALITY

We are ultimately made of energy. Every thought, every feeling, and every emotion leaves our human energy field and ripples out into the Universe. Communication never ceases. The interconnectedness between the messages we send and the principles and laws of the Universe are absolute. Our thoughts, feelings, and emotions carry more weight and consequence than you might possibly imagine. There are lots of sayings on the topic, "What you think about you bring about", "You are the sum total of all your thoughts", "Thoughts create reality", "Thoughts are things and things matter", and then there is even more wisdom to behold,

"Your beliefs become your thoughts,
Your thoughts become your words,
Your words become your actions,
Your actions become your habits,
Your habits become your values,
Your values become your destiny." -
 -Mahatma Ghandi

I would like to personally insert, Your values become your character and Your character becomes your destiny.

The Law of Attraction is widely misunderstood- when its power is believed to pull things to you- attract things to you. Have you wondered why you haven't been able to manifest the things you want? Have you ever muttered, "This Law of Attraction thing doesn't work..." If you have, it's because you may have missed the real underlying cause and effect that the Law of Attraction operates with.

It is only when you achieve the level of consciousness required to experience the fruit of your desires will you be able to see them in your reality. You already have everything! In other words, you already have what you desire. There is nothing to attract but you must consciously be a match, and when you are, you will be given new eyesight to see it in your reality.

"I know for sure, what we dwell on, is who we become".
--Oprah Winfrey

The fullness of who we become, is entirely up to us. We have so many choices. So many opportunities to succeed... But we don't see it that way sometimes because of our awareness of our current conditions, the assessment of where we are right now- WITHOUT the things we so desperately want. We look around, and it doesn't look like the life we chose or would choose...

Here is the piece that makes both children and adults cry; we don't get to have the experience of instant gratification! Inside each and every one of us is a desire for instant gratification but the energetic system for manifestation has built in safety nets to make sure we don't manifest every thought we think – otherwise the world would be even more chaotic than it already appears. Children hold the key to remind us how we can manifest with less resistance. Children are usually much better at manifesting than adults since they go after what they want fearlessly and relentlessly, fully expecting to get what they want. Adults tend to put up resistance in the form of negative thoughts and self talk.

What is little known and not fully understood by most is that what appears in our current reality are actually old thoughts made manifest. Like the wake of a boat, our previous thoughts that are attached to current manifestations are always trailing behind our present moment thoughts and beliefs which creates the illusion "this is the way it is" in our current reality. REREAD this last sentence over and over until it is fully understood.

This had me confused and stuck for a very long time after watching the movie "The Secret". I thought if I could think positively, meditate on my vision board, and emotionalize what it was to actually have what I desired, that 'shazaam' they would manifest in my reality. This is partly true but it's missing some critical components making it only PART of the story.

I did not understand the concept that my current conditions were simply old thoughts- therefore it would be wise not to give those thoughts about my current conditions power if they differed from what I desired, and it would be best to just accept them for what they are- just old thoughts! That I needed to focus my attention on only the good things in my conditions and show immense gratitude for them while continuing to focus my thoughts and emotions on the new vision for my life. I think the trap is not fully understanding the principles and laws governing physical manifestation and the concept of PATIENCE and MANAGING RESISTANCE as it relates to them.

It is so easy to fall into a vicious cycle of- positive thinking, followed by resistant thoughts because we don't see a change in our conditions, followed by disappointment, followed by renewed hope, followed by positive thoughts, followed by resistant thoughts because our conditions STILL haven't changed- we STILL don't have what we want... and on and on. This is important to both understand and acknowledge this cycle. Many of us have found ourselves on this hamster wheel. It is very difficult to get off the hamster wheel because of the level of patience required to wait it out. Patience is a virtue. Patience goes against instant gratification that we are hard-wired for. Patience is something we need to cultivate and the best way to do that is to restore our faith in the perfect unfolding of our desires.

Now let's bust the myth, "You can't always have what you want!" You can have what you want through conscious creation (creating your greatest good that is in alignment with your divine life blueprint), and there is a way that you can operate with the principles and laws that get you what you want. The first step is doing the work to connect with Source energy (God). The second step is establishing your values and truths and mapping your highest vision. The third step is gratitude. Always be grateful for the good in your life, from the biggest of blessings right down to the smallest things we typically take for granted. Then the following steps will help guide you to successful manifestations in creating that which you desire:

Step 1- Get very clear about what you want and write it down.
 Step 2- Commit to a daily practice to give it attention and feel into it with emotion.

(Pray knowing that you have received- Give thanks)

Step 3- Clear guidance will come to you on how to take action, TAKE ACTION and don't procrastinate.
Step 4- Throughout the day allow yourself the excitement of its impending arrival.
Step 5- When you have a thought that is negative/resistant stop yourself - Say to it "you're an old belief, I don't need you anymore".
Step 6- Override the resistant thought with your new belief that you will have it and remind yourself of why you want it.
Rinse and repeat (It's not a 1 and done)
Step 7- Exercise patience giving no power to your current conditions or appearances.
Step 8- Express gratitude in your daily practice, praying that you have received it in the spiritual realm and it is now making its way to the physical realm.

REPEAT STEPS 7 & 8 strengthening your Belief every day... until you have it.

Gratitude and Patience are critical components to manifesting that which you desire. This is a worthy process to commit to when creating your reality. This is what it means to "overcome the illusions of the world" by giving no power to your current conditions. This is the only way someone takes themselves out of debt, out of bad relationships, out of a disease within their body, out of poverty and lack.

The biggest obstacles to success are usually 3 things: not knowing what you want, not taking action, and persistent resistant thoughts that you don't have a process to manage. The mile between your desires and bringing them into reality are completely dependent on your ability to manage resistant thoughts. Your resistant thoughts are the only thing in your way. YOU are the only thing in your way. There are no adverse forces at play keeping you separated from what you want. This is an illusion that you and many others have bought into, including myself until I learned otherwise.

We are powerful beyond measure. The great masters that came before and those that are here now are reminding us to wake up to this truth. We were born knowing, we simply have to do the work to raise our consciousness and step into our 'knowingness'. When you ask for something, you are immediately answered in the spiritual dimension, and the answer is always YES (so be careful what you ask for). It will stay in that dimension as 'spiritual escrow' until you create a matching vibration to manifest it in the physical dimension. We have all spent years and sometimes lifetimes creating an escrow of overflowing abundance, that is never made manifest. The inner work that you can embark on right now can change all that. Raising your vibration requires clearing any blocks you may have and developing a practice to keep you tuned in to your Higher power and that which you desire. You are supported. Your soul, God, the Universe and the Angels have only one response to ALL that you choose, "and so it is".

When you acknowledge that you are indeed the creator of your life, you are no longer a victim of anything that has held you back. The difficult and painful things will lose their significance and you will stop creating more of the same experiences.

Do not be hard on yourself for previous creations. When you can accept full responsibility for all of your creations you will begin to see the needs for your soul's development that have surfaced in the form of people and experiences. Take the lessons and leave the rest behind.

LET GO OF YOUR PAST. God keeps no record of the past for His energy exists only in the ever present NOW. So you should follow suit and keep no record of your mistakes or anyone else's. That doesn't mean that anyone can go out and commit "bad deeds" any time they want with no consequences. There are other Laws of the Universe in place for that, like the Law of Karma. Our character depends on our ability to stay true to our values.

Tim McGraw is one of my favorite musicians. He and his wife, Faith Hill embody "character" and the "power of love" through their music. My favorite song of Tim's is "Humble and Kind". The lyrics so engaging that he used them to create his first book. Here are just a few of the lyrics…

Hold the door, say please, say thank you
Don't steal, don't cheat, and don't lie
 I know you got mountains to climb but
Always stay humble and kind

When the dreams you're dreamin' come to you
When the work you put in is realized
Let yourself feel the pride but
Always stay humble and kind

Don't expect a free ride from no one
Don't hold a grudge or a chip and here's why
Bitterness keeps you from flyin'
Always stay humble and kind

Don't take for granted the love this life gives you
When you get where you're goin
Don't forget turn back around
And help the next one in line
Always stay humble and kind

CHAPTER 10
YOUR BIGGEST DREAM

Before you were born into this world you were given a vision, a vision of the fullest potential of your life- your biggest dream. Prepared to succeed you came to the Earth willing to play full out and realize that dream. Then, somewhere along the way, an impostor named FEAR took over and got the best of you.

"Our deepest fear is not that we are inadequate. Our deepest fear is that we are powerful beyond measure. It is our light, not our darkness that most frightens us. We ask ourselves, Who am I to be brilliant, gorgeous, talented, and fabulous? Actually, who are you not to be? You are a child of God. Your playing small does not serve the world. There is nothing enlightened about shrinking so that other people will not feel insecure around you. We are all meant to shine, as children do. We were born to make manifest the glory of God that is within us. It is not just in some of us; it is in everyone and as we let our own light shine, we unconsciously give others permission to do the same. As we are liberated from our own fear, our presence automatically liberates others."
 -Marianne Williamson

It's time to eliminate fear (an illusion) and live into your biggest dream. You're never too young or too old to want it or experience it. What is time anyways? In our minds we hold the same inspirations and desires to be all that we came to be, no matter what age we are.

Your life IS like a movie with you playing the starring role. You get to script it from start to finish and decide what character you will play and what the storyline will be. If you were given an exercise to write your script, would you have writer's block? You might... If you do, this would be a good time to start a daily practice where you connect with your Higher power and let the messages and guidance surface within you. It's also important to note that you and only you have specific preferences for EVERYTHING based on who you came to be and what you came to do... so follow your intuition... and follow your joy as your Internal Guidance System steers the way.

If you were able to put pen to paper, what would you write? Would you be too embarrassed to give yourself the role of having everything you ever wanted? Don't cut yourself short, as it is your very birthright to want what you want in this lifetime. What would you choose if you were a billionaire, had nothing to fear or lose and were completely safe? This 1 question alone will take you in the vicinity of your biggest dream. Let your imagination safely soar because the only possibilities that will surface will be those that you were born with. They were divinely inspired and they are seeking to be born with every breath you take.

Will you allow the fullest potential of yourself to emerge? Will you give up control of the process? The apple tree doesn't try to grow pears. The caterpillar doesn't try to change its external conditions to find its freedom as a butterfly. It patiently awaits the unfolding of a perfect process. TRUST the process. Trust that the Laws of the Universe also have dominion over your life!

The Free Will that we possess as humans is the main difference between the perfect unfolding of the acorn becoming the oak tree or the caterpillar becoming the butterfly and us; we have the potential to screw it up or slow it down. It will be to the degree that you will allow the unfolding of your life that your potential will be realized. In other words, picture a long string of cutout paper dolls (male or female). The first paper doll in the string is completely resistant to trusting and allowing the perfect unfolding of his/her life. The last paper doll is completely in full realization of his/her potential at any given moment in time. All of the dolls in between are on the sliding scale of potentiality. Where are you on the scale? Who would you have to become consciously to realize your full potential? Wherever you fall on the sliding scale to your full potential- this is the work yet to be done.

CHAPTER 11
GRATITUDE

"He is a wise man who does not grieve for the things which he has not, but rejoices for those which he has."
-Epictetus

Until we express gratitude for that which we have in our lives, nothing new can enter. This is a principle that would be well worth its recognition. Forget your conditions (if they displease you), the seeming appearances that surround you, for they are temporary. There is more in the midst of your environment that does deserve your attention. You will be able to find more than a hundred things to be grateful for right now, right where you are. There is no greater heart medicine than thankfulness, thankfulness for the things that you do have and for the things that you will have soon. It is the path of no resistance to well-being, and it is yours for the taking.

"You simply will not be the same person two months from now after consciously giving thanks each day for the abundance that exists in your life. And you will have set in motion an ancient spiritual law: the more you have and are grateful for, the more will be given you."

If consciously we know that by raising our vibration we will be able to witness an abundant world, where we already have everything, then by definition the only thing that is missing from our lives is that which we are not consciously pouring forth or giving. Derek Rydall's "Awakened Wealth" program and his book and podcasts on "The Law of Emergence" offer up the best articulation on why something is missing in your life and how you can get it. He consistently says, "The only thing missing from your life is that which you aren't giving! For example, if you don't have enough love, you need to give more love. If you don't have enough money, you need to give more money. If you want better relationships, you need to be a better partner or friend."

It is an inside-out projection, not the other way around. If you understand this principle, it becomes easier to resolve issues in these fundamental areas of your life. If you do only 1 thing - express gratitude daily in the form of unconditional giving, your life will change in remarkable ways! How I envision gratitude... Gratitude is the fountain of youth whereby all our innocence and humility pour forth into sparkling droplets of grace, and the wisdom contained therein has the power to keep us forever young. Like the fountain, our love is continuously being circulated from person to person and from generation to generation.

Be grateful for this life, count your blessings and give thanks to God for who you are right now and who you are in the process of becoming- for you are a divine spark of His perfection!

CHAPTER 12
A DAILY PRACTICE

When I turned the corner to becoming more grateful for all of the people and things in my life- down to the tiniest of things, my life opened up. I searched long and hard to try and find a way to hold onto the feeling of gratitude and to find a path to facilitate and nurture the changes I knew I needed to make- that's when I discovered a daily practice. A ritual, whereby I found my power and its true source, from which many truths were revealed, and perfect guidance was delivered and continues to be delivered on a daily basis.

We can find clues in a word.
Spi**ritual** contains the word ritual.

Rituals create sacred space. We all need sacred space, sacred space to enrich our souls and grow in consciousness. Rituals provide a safe haven to imagine with our mind, create through our thoughts, and manifest into reality everything we want in this lifetime.
Since the beginning of time rituals have played a major role in humanity. A ritual is a ceremonious act that grounds us to the Earth yet allows our Spirits to soar. Rituals contain no barriers, no boundaries, no

borders... they happen everywhere and anywhere a human Spirit reaches for joy.

Once I discovered the treasure of a ritual- a daily practice, I knew I had found the answer to a lifetime of longing, a longing to commune with my Creator and be shown His vision for my life. Through this ritual I was able to unearth a golden path, a path of consciousness that unravels the mysteries of life so that I am able to see more clearly who I am and why I'm here.

As a result, I am not the same person as I was prior to this practice. I have changed in profound ways and continue to change as my consciousness grows. It is this practice that showed me a vision for my future and gave me clear guidance to take my first steps toward it. I believe this is the "new awakening" taking place one by one as we move toward a more conscious Earth.

My greatest joy is to share with you this ritual, a daily practice that I created called Power Practice 365. It's a practice whereby your biggest questions find answers, your fears and doubts are laid to rest, and you arrive in a place that allows you to transition to a more powerful "You" and create the life you were designed for. Through this practice you will come to the realization you already have everything... and by harnessing your power you can manifest everything you want by developing your soul and growing your consciousness. If you do the inner work to raise your vibration you will finally be able to experience, and see with your own eyes, what's waiting for you- and it will be far more than you ever expected or imagined...

I went to an intuitive 7 years ago who told me I would write a book on spirituality and would eventually teach it. It resonated with me at the time but I kept waiting for the words to surface. Why did I hesitate? Quite possibly because of a subconscious desire to have longer residency in the School of Hard Knocks so that I could relate in an intimate way with the crises listed in this book. So that I could cover more ground on how and where a person can get stuck in trying to manifest their desires. So that I would be inspired to create a daily practice for my own well-being...so that Power Practice 365 could be born and that I could offer it to anyone wanting its treasures.

Regardless of how long it took for me to write this book, I can now take you to a place that took me years to get to. It is my purpose and mission to share this practice with as many people as I can because of its power to develop the soul and raise consciousness.

You too can gain clarity and confidence around your biggest dream- your purpose and mission, more satisfying relationships, optimal health, increased finances, and a solid faith that brings peace. You too can gain a powerful process to commune with your

Creator or simply participate in a ritual that allows for your best day every day to consciously unfold. You can excavate your authentic self and step into your power. You will STEP IN (do the practice) STEP UP (raise your consciousness and vibration) and STEP OUT (renewed and reenergized). You are powerful and this practice will affirm it day in and day out.

Just by seeing the structure of a daily practice-whether you use Power Practice 365 or simply want to create your own daily ritual, you will have a practice to develop your soul. I have found that it works best to establish the practice as a morning ritual. It is an opportunity to start each day with a powerful mindset and clear focus for everything you would like to achieve. When I created Power Practice 365 I intuitively extracted the following core principles…

POWER PRACTICE 365 CORE PRINCIPLES

At the center of any Great Life,
is ongoing soul development.

At the core of any Great Person,
is higher consciousness.

The foundation of any Great Day,
is super--conscious awareness.

POWER PRACTICE 365
DAILY PRACTICE CORE COMPONENTS

-MEDI-PRAYER
(PRAYER WITHIN MEDITATION)
(Includes a 'how to' video)

-DIVINE LIFE BLUEPRINT

-IMAGES

-DECK OF AFFIRMATIONS

-AUDIO YOUR BIGGEST DREAM

-GRATITUDE JOURNAL

There are 8 modules with a curriculum to understand the components of a daily practice. In addition it includes a soul detox & cleanse exercise, medi-prayer instructions, modalities for manifesting, and a step-by-step guide to establishing a powerful daily practice. It is offered via Private or Group Coaching.

This practice honors God (Source Energy). It's a daily commitment to commune and have a deeply focused awareness of His presence. All of the answers to all of our questions lie within through our connection to Source. And the promise, "if you seek, you shall find" could never be truer through a commitment to a daily practice.

CHAPTER 13
MANAGING RESISTANCE

Resistance. As humans we have it and whether we are aware of it or not, it's blocking our growth and soul development. We have somewhere between 40,000 and 60,000 thoughts per day with over 90% of them the same as the thoughts we had the day before, and of those daily thoughts approximately 80% of them are negative. With this data, it is no wonder that the game of manifesting is a difficult one indeed. I pointed out earlier that the mile between our desires and their manifestation depends on managing resistant thoughts. Resistant thoughts by their very nature have the power to keep you from your goals and dreams.

So how do you manage the bombardment of so many negative thoughts? Well for starters, become intimately aware of your thoughts. Make a point to observe what it is that you are spending large blocks of time thinking about in the course of your day. At this stage you are simply getting a handle on your current thoughts. Secondly, decide to step out of the statistic. Just because people have on average 40,000 negative thoughts doesn't mean that you have to be one of them. Statistics are simply numbers and they only have power when you believe in their possibility to control your destiny. The staggering statistic that around 90% of small businesses fail doesn't mean that you have to fail too, if you are pursuing your passion through entrepreneurship.

Once you become aware of your thoughts - the negative self talk, write them down, and then look long and hard at your biggest dream. Compare and contrast your actual thoughts to the very thoughts that would get you in alignment vibrationally with your dream. Therein lies the work that needs to be done- close the gap between what is it that you want and your 'thoughts' about what it is that you want.

Next step is to remain aware of your thoughts as they come up. When a negative thought enters - sit with it for a moment and don't judge it. It's not really important whether it is right or wrong per se, it's simply an old belief that you no longer consider true and you'll be replacing it with a new belief. Then read an affirmation or say one to yourself silently affirming the new belief that you WILL have what it is that you want.

When you start each morning with a daily practice it gets you immediately into a state of mind that produces "helpful thoughts" and makes it easier to greatly reduce the number of negative thoughts and negative self-talk. It just feels wrong to commune with our Creator, be given perfect guidance and then think negative thoughts about our lives! Instead, you will experience good feelings and emotions that propel you in the direction of your desires. Perfect guidance flows to assist in the next step on the staircase to right action that moves you toward your goals.

Another way to reduce negative thoughts is to spend time doing things that you love. If you spend time doing the very things that bring you joy and therefore activate a higher vibration, you will have nice big blocks of time that will only allow for positive thoughts to enter.

"He enjoys true leisure ,
who has time,
to improve his soul's estate."
-Henry David Thoreau

Strive to be happy! The following shortlist is a reminder of the activities or things you can do, and when done consciously keep away resistant thoughts from entering: (in no particular order)
Prayer
Meditation
Laughter
Enjoying a meal with your family or friends
Spending time in nature
Playing
Listening to music

Singing
Writing
Painting
Playing a sport
Dancing
Gardening
Cooking
Playing with your dog or pet
Watching an inspirational movie
Reading an inspirational book
Reading your biggest dream or divine life blueprint
Spending time at the beach
Enjoying the sunshine
Boating
Enjoying the stars at night
Lighting a bunch of candles
Traveling to new places
Learning something new
Creating & building
And so on...

If you can be proactive with your thoughts instead of reactive, you will have the ability to dramatically reduce the number of negative thoughts you process. When you operate on a daily basis with purpose, have a mission and a plan, your focus shifts to "building" instead of "tearing down". With practice, it becomes easier and easier, and is accompanied by more and more recognizable signs of validation that you're on the right path.

CHAPTER 14
SPEAKING YOUR TRUTH

Once you have established a daily practice, greatly reduced your negative thoughts and have reclaimed your power, powerful truths will emerge as they pertain to every single area of your life. By communing with our Creator on a daily basis you will step into your authentic self and begin to remember the truths you were born with. It will feel amazing! It is a soul cleansing and detox that serves to get rid of every single thing you picked up on your journey that no longer serves you. You will then fill back up with pure love and the vision of who you came to be.

You will feel like shouting from the rooftops, "I found it!" and as a result, you will begin to share with your inner circle your breakthroughs in consciousness. You will be tested. Some will be thrilled by your growth... others will play their role:) and challenge you at every turn. You will be required to speak your truth with articulation and stand your ground. View each attack (sometimes it can feel like that) as yet another opportunity to practice speaking your truth. You will also receive internal feedback. If you are solid in your truth you will begin to feel a wonderful sensation, a hit from your Internal Guidance System that brings you joy. You will have validation that you are on your way to more confidence and greater clarity than ever before.

As you continue to get stronger, you will be put in ever-greater situations that create opportunities to speak your truth. Take them head on. If you are a person that cares about what others think of you and you place importance on others' projections; speaking your truth will feel liberating. Once you have the ability to stand your ground and speak your truth about the things that are important to you, you will no longer care what others think... This is what it means to truly love yourself- all parts of yourself no matter what's being projected on to you. Your primary relationship is between you and your Creator and all other relationships flow from there. There is freedom in this truth.

CHAPTER 15
9 INSIGHTS FROM THE
CELESTINE PROPHECY
James Redfield

1

We are discovering again that we live in a deeply
mysterious world, full of sudden coincidences and
synchronistic encounters that seem destined.

2

As more of us awaken to this mystery, we will create a
completely new Worldview - redefining the Universe as
energetic and sacred.

3

We will discover that everything around us, all matter,
consists of and stems from a Divine energy that we are
beginning to see and understand.

4

From this perspective, we can see that humans have
always felt insecure and disconnected from this sacred
source, and have tried to take energy by dominating

each other. This struggle is responsible for all human conflict.

5

The only solution is to cultivate a personal reconnection with the Divine, a mystical transformation that fills us with unlimited energy and love, extends our perception of beauty, and lifts us into a higher self-awareness.

6

In this awareness, we can release our own pattern of controlling, and discover a specific truth, a mission, we are here to share that helps evolve humanity toward this new level reality.

7

In pursuit of this mission, we can discover an inner intuition that shows us where to go and what to do, and if we make only positive interpretations, brings a flow of coincidences that opens the door for our mission to unfold.

8

When enough of us enter this evolutionary flow, always giving energy to the higher self of everyone we meet, we will build a new culture where our bodies evolve to ever-higher levels of energy and perception.

9

In this way, we participate in the long journey of evolution from the Big Bang to life's ultimate goal: to energize our bodies, Generation by Generation until we walk into a Heaven we can finally see.

Once you increase your awareness and shift to a higher consciousness, your perceptions will shift in ways that bring you peace. The world will appear to be more colorful, as if the lens to your eyes has been switched to a more capable and higher quality lens.

CHAPTER 16
RELEASE & SURRENDER

It is the title of this book. It was chosen for the title for its ability to create miracles, miracles that forever change the course of a person's life.

Our world is filled with dichotomies. There is possibly no greater example than the dichotomy of Free Will. Release & Surrender are located on its opposite axis and both are absolutely essential to the human experience. It may be considered a balancing mechanism when one or the other is taken to the extreme but this I know for sure, when Free Will is exercised through unconscious creations, we will eventually and most certainly be forced to release and surrender. Release and surrender to a much wiser truth that when we learn to create consciously, we create only that which is in our greatest good.

Releasing and surrendering is part of the path to higher consciousness and it will require dismantling certain beliefs that no longer serve you. This can be a painful process. Everyone has a pain story and a progress story. You will be able to live into your progress story faster if you don't resist the process. I repeatedly kept getting the same lesson in a different costume until I figured out what was really happening. I kept unconsciously creating experiences that brought me the lesson- to finally then become conscious of the lesson, accept it, smile at it, transcend it, and move on to create consciously in that area of my life.

We all have blind spots. You can count on family, friends and sometimes complete strangers to bring you the lesson when you are ready. If you realize that you are in fact the one creating your experiences then you will also realize that whomever it is that is bringing you the lesson, they are providing the service you requested. There is no need to become angry, judgmental or afraid. It just becomes one more thing to work through and add to your soul's development.

I named the book Release & Surrender because it is one of the hardest things to do. The very nature of it being on the opposite pole of Free Will makes it so. In the middle you'll find peace... for both ends of the spectrum will require you to center yourself in God. When you act from this place, when you create from this place, you'll realize your dream, the dream you came to the Earth with.

The surrendered life is one that fully embraces love as the focus for every encounter and situation. Surrender means surrendering to a Higher power that knows best how to guide its own creation. Surrendering means taking right action without having to know the outcome. How joyous life becomes when we just let go!

If we can act on perfect guidance and stay in the mystery of what tomorrow brings - we can experience synchronicity at the highest level, synchronicities that fill in the blanks of our divine life blueprint and propel us toward the magnificent life we know in our hearts is possible. As we release fear and exercise faith in the universal laws and principles and surrender to the very process we see as perfect in nature, we begin to experience a freedom unlike anything we've experienced before.

CHAPTER 17
FREEDOM

The new awakening toward a more conscious Earth is happening right now as more and more people seek deeper purpose and meaning in their lives- and seek a specific mission to give their lives to. This seeking creates a desire to commune with our Creator in a consistent way for guidance, direction and heightened awareness. The promise offered is a golden path that paves the way to being free.

Freedom embodies many qualities - love, passion, joy, excitement, pleasure, contentment, and the list goes on. When attained it is the perfect peace, the last frontier, the Holy Grail.

We all deserve to be free. Free to know the truth about who we are and why we're here. Free to be ourselves- stripped of all masks and armor. Free to follow divine inspiration with zero resistance. Free to realize our biggest dream.

As each person makes their way to being free, the collective consciousness inches its way closer to freedom. If we choose to do our part- play our role- we attain our birthright, the freedom to live into the highest and fullest expressions of ourselves. And in the process experience maximal love, peace and joy.

Our intention is a worthy one… to leave a legacy of freedom for generations to come while honoring our Source and the sacred dimension. If we could lift the veil for even a moment, we would fall deeply in love. The beautiful forces of compassion, joy, love and equanimity swirling around and dancing amongst us everywhere; if only our senses were evolved enough to see.

CHAPTER 18
THE MEANING OF MIRACLES
From A Course in Miracles
Foundation for Inner Peace

There is profound wisdom written on the pages of the book, "A Course in Miracles". The following are just a few of the Principles of Miracles:

-There is no order of difficulty in miracles. One is not "harder" or "bigger" than another. They are all the same. All expressions of love are maximal.

-Miracles as such do not matter. The only thing that matters is their Source, which is far beyond evaluation.

-Miracles occur naturally as expressions of love. The real miracle is the love that inspires them. In this sense everything that comes from love is a miracle.

-All miracles mean life, and God is the giver of life. His voice will direct you very specifically. You will be told all you need to know.

-Miracles are everyone's right, but purification is necessary first.

-Miracles are healing because they supply a lack; they are performed by those who temporarily have more for those who temporarily have less.

-Prayer is the medium of miracles. It is a means of communication of the created with the Creator. Through prayer love is received, and through miracles love is expressed.

-Miracles are teaching devices for demonstrating it is as blessed to give as to receive. They simultaneously increase the strength of the giver and supply strength to the receiver.

-Miracles reawaken the awareness that the spirit, not the body, is the altar of truth. This is the recognition that leads to the healing power of the miracle.

-Miracles are part of an interlocking chain of forgiveness which, when completed, is the Atonement. Atonement works all the time and in all the dimensions of time.

-Miracles represent freedom from fear. "Atoning" means "undoing". The undoing of fear is an essential part of the Atonement value of miracles.

-Miracles praise God through you. They praise him by honoring His creations, affirming their perfection. They heal because they deny body-identification and affirm spirit-identification.

-By recognizing spirit, miracles adjust the levels of perception and show them in proper alignment. This places spirit at the center, where it can communicate directly.

-Miracles should inspire gratitude, not awe. You should thank God for what you really are. The children of God are holy and the miracle honors their holiness, which can be hidden but never lost.

-Miracles honor you because you are lovable. They dispel illusions about yourself and perceive the light in you. They thus atone for your errors by freeing you from your nightmares. By releasing your mind from the imprisonment of your illusions, they restore your sanity.

-The miracle acknowledges everyone as your brother and mine. It is a way of perceiving the universal mark of God.

The Will of God is One and all there is. This is your heritage. The universe beyond the sun and stars, and all of the thoughts of which you can conceive, belong to you.

God's peace is the condition for His Will. Attain His peace,
and you remember Him.

———————————————

Release & Surrender to God and the Universe.

IT'S YOUR TURN FOR A MIRACLE.

-End-

"Be the change that you wish to see in the world." -
-Ghandi

ABOUT THE AUTHOR

Visit DeborahNaone.com

Deborah Naone is an Author, Spiritual Life Coach, Speaker and Mother of 2 whose purpose and mission is to participate in raising the consciousness of the planet. Her work experiences diverse- both entrepreneurial and corporate. It is her extensive work and travel experiences that have contributed to her soul's development and her Coaching Practice.

As a Spiritual Life Coach, Deborah assists her Clients to raise their consciousness in order to experience abundance and a deeper meaning in their lives. She's results-driven while providing warmth and compassion to those seeking clarity in building a solid foundation for their Mission, Relationships, Health, Finances and Faith. Technology allows her to coach anyone in the world no matter his or her geographic location.

Deborah Naone is the Author of the following Titles available on Amazon:

RITUAL JOURNAL SERIES FOR
SOUL DEVELOPMENT (The Perfect Gift)

"OUR LOVE STORY Relationship Journal"
"BUCKET LIST Ritual Journal"
"FIRESIDE Ritual Journal"
"GRATITUDE Ritual Journal"
"HUNT & GATHER Ritual Journal"

She is the creator of the program "Power Practice 365", a daily practice to develop the soul and raise consciousness.

She is the founder of Conscious Business Mavericks, an International movement of Generation Y Millennials, "The Next Great Generation". She strongly believes in providing resources to young adults in an effort to facilitate their spiritual growth and fast track their way to the pursuit of their mission, whether it is entrepreneurship or other paths- to ultimately experience fuller and richer lives of abundance while giving back to humanity.

COACHING SERVICES

Private Coaching via Skype or Phone
(Global Clients)
Power Practice 365 - Private / Group Coaching
Power Practice 365 for the Workplace

Plus free Inspirational Resources & Information available on her website.

www.DeborahNaone.com

17274564R00071

Printed in Poland
by Amazon Fulfillment
Poland Sp. z o.o., Wrocław